AF265377

memoir

piers laurent

memoir

Copyright © 2018 by Piers Laurent

All rights reserved; no part of this publication may be reproduced, stored in a retrieval system, or transmitted in any form or by any means (electronic, mechanical, photocopying, recording, or otherwise) without the prior written permission of the author or publisher except in the case of reprints in the context of reviews.

The moral right of the author has been asserted.

ISBN: 978-0-9959410-7-6

This print edition first published in 2018.

The names, characters, places, and incidents depicted in this work may be the product of the author's imagination, be used fictitiously, be dramatized for narrative purposes, or have been changed for privacy reasons. Thus, in certain cases, if not all, any resemblance to actual persons, living or deceased, business establishments, events, or locales is purely coincidental.

Thank you for buying an authorized edition of this book and for complying with copyright laws. You are supporting writers and publishers, allowing them to continue creating content for every reader.

as i lie in bed
next to the one i cherish
i cannot help but reflect on
the past relationships
and experiences
that have led me here

contents

memoir

the first

part one

piers laurent

the blissful days of our youthful years
nothing of importance but having fun
the first time i witnessed your presence
high above us beamed the bright sun

tanned skin so radiant and glowing
hair in braids with beads at the end
that first moment my eyes went to you
i wanted to be more than a friend

— *at first sight*

a spunky youth you ran wild and free
dressed in rags though still so lovely
clothes torn and stained for all to see
no matter the wear you were sightly

— *attraction*

while at first i was rather shy
each passing day i would try
have you take a liking to me
a couple was all i wanted to be

— *dreams of the young*

cheers to the many hours
head so stuck in the clouds
the mind wandering curiously
thoughts keen to overcrowd

— daydreaming about you

a striking sight to be seen
a shift of brown to green

a gnawing feeling in my core
said there was something more

beyond the window was a secret
your soul dwelt in concealment

— eyes telling a tale

i saw the pain fear and bore
of which your eyes wore

the life holding you back
leading you off track

tears hoping to be set free
yet you never showed me

— *hiding*

i wanted you to open your chest
show me the look of your heart
for you to tell me your story
every word from the very start

i wanted you to lean against me
explain the ailing of your soul
why did you become so empty
when you were surely once whole

— confess to me

a lost cause you truly were
always in search of a remedy
for the pain that was tormenting
and i unaware how to handle
followed so you would be with me

— pernicious bonding

you told me not to worry
entranced i listened

you were there with me
delighted i smiled

you took the first puff
when i held up the light

that moment was enough
excitement to last the night

— *blazed*

your hurting i neglected
so we could be united
each time we connected

— *being selfish*

exploring time and time again
new memories to never end
when reality crept upon us
we let our minds transcend

— *ecstasy*

but your pain remained
hindering our progression
we became stagnant while
committing transgressions

— *stuck*

a hobby of yours became mine
one i engaged in quite a few times
how silly of me to feel
that if we shared an interest
i would be seen as less of a pest

— *foolish me*

abandoned in the dark on my own
to fend for myself all alone
mind tweaked and eyes seeing lights
senseless yet joyous during the night

— *stars in the eyes*

and even when you did me wrong
i was never one to give up on you

— *i tried*

most times when i was there
your mind was elsewhere

— *unfocused*

a single call and i arrived in a flash
walked you home on the coldest of days
picked you up whenever down
though still i was always kept at bay
stuck at a range feeling so far away

— *lengthy distance*

i was kept around as merely a toy
to have easy access to in your world
a living figurine for you to destroy

— *dollhouse*

how idiotic of me
to worry whether we
had a feeling to share
as if you cared

— conflicted

every part of me longed
for us to have another moment
you were never one to disagree
surely it elevated your enjoyment

— *deadly second chances*

you drowned your sadness and pain
with elation and instant gratification

played with your good health
a fool i was for my dedication

my mind awoke before too late
your chaos caused my ruination

in desperate need to rid your toxins
yet your goal was domination

— *detox*

a repetitive game of cat and mouse
going back and forth again again
a dangerous road to arrive at
parting ways was a matter of when

— *difficult choices*

even the weak find strength
regardless the length
to do what must be done
break from a poisonous one

— in search of a cure

only when i walked away forever
did you embark on new endeavours
i was to have none of it whatsoever
from you i learned to be more clever

— *getting educated*

the distance in your eyes
a look of defeat and death
of no longer wanting to try

no warning signs given
for the change you were about to make
actions to which you felt driven

it was then sadly the end
had you confessed your suffering
never would you have had to pretend

in an instant you disappeared
a slit to the wrist in a tub of water
never again did i see you my dear

— *unfortunate ending*

blood poured from its host
a view as vivid as
spilled wine upon a white carpet
an image as clear as
red paint stained on a blank canvas
a tragic scene when seen
though still a work of art
truly a masterpiece

— *beautiful disaster*

29

the second

part two

piers laurent

in the darkest corner of my room
where i sat feeling intense gloom

in the darkest area of my life
great despair cut at me like a knife

in the darkest corner ever to be seen
sulking in a small place so unclean

in the darkest area where i remained
i waited a long time feeling drained

— *sorrow*

i had become the broken one
confined as my misery begun
going about the days trapped
in my own prison of no escape
surrounded by blackness

— *gloom*

a beating heart so youthful
should it ever be so hurt
still tender and vulnerable
where was my timely alert

— *young and in pain*

when least expected
a spark was detected

a ripple ran through my veins
and in that darkest time
i then felt alive and quite sane

the moment our eyes locked
a jolt of electricity
awoke my senses with a shock

— *resurrection*

a surge of virility rushed
through warm red blood
spilling out my pores easily
quickly causing a flood

— *dripping in excitement*

park benches near the river
a slight breeze to cause a shiver

petals and leaves in the water
a preferred location to wander

cloudless skies and bright rays
the sun so radiant in the day

the many nice afternoons
before the month of june

— *spring dating*

but something was not right
despite wanting to overlook it

excitement built up evermore
then crashed down afterwards

down and up and up and down
high speeds from all around

— *roller coaster*

behind the blissful moments
what i hoped to not be true
something was wrong and i knew

behind the blissful moments
cracks i hoped would mend
so what we had would not end

— *beyond the allure*

first moments it felt meant to be
you were the epitome of ideal
i danced to the sound of your voice
smiled and i knew you rejoiced
but a nice sound turned to bad noise

— *lower the volume*

what i was told in a tone quite solemn
that i was at fault for every problem

the sole creator of a powerful poison
the initiator making your blood boil and

the one who started every argument
the reason we were not permanent

— *at blame*

you said that i was crazy
and a crazy never knows
who they really are

you orchestrated ploys
hoping to prove a point
desperate to leave scars

— *scheming*

i was always one to admit
when doing something wrong
all you hoped to accomplish
was showing me i did not belong

— *flawed*

never did i simply blame you
for all the shit i went through
i realized i had my part to play
so at the end of any dark days
the word *sorry* i made sure to say

— *accepting responsibility*

and still i continued to do wrong
my feelings sunk too hard to explain
words only known in a sad love song

— *your perspective of me*

shall we start anew
i was confident saying

something you agreed to
and went along playing

again the same situations
happened over and over

rather foolish occasions
which provided no closure

— *erase rewind repeat*

it was done
oh how we knew
you faded away
so suddenly one day

— *vanished*

47

the third

part three

piers laurent

that wide grin you shined
one so apparently innocent
yet something felt unpleasant
unsettling in my mind

— *uneasy encounter*

first impressions are bullshit
so i gave a chance to a misfit

— *being hopeful*

shown to be kind and generous
with every single act
yet your true self was venomous
quickly shown to be a fact

— *thespian*

to most it would have been viewed
as a warning sign so clear to see
that the many offerings you had given
were something more than generosity

your persistence to give me the world
your insistence for me to take it all
forced me to begin wondering
if there would be a quick downfall

— *endless gifting*

every evening you made contact
late response and you acted out

you asked about my location
questioned my whereabouts
no answer was good enough
you always had your doubts

every evening you made contact
no response and you acted out

you made claims of my doings
was convinced i was a cheat
that i was a horrible person
my words stained with deceit

— *your insecurities*

you wanted to always be together
like we were meant to be tethered

you aspired to break me
of my normal habits
something you often said so boldly

you longed to steer me
away from myself
to who you thought i should be

— *controlling*

how stupid of me to believe
that what i had dealt with was
the worst

the bad only progressed
so unpleasant with each coming
outburst

— *from bad to worse*

i was in a complex state
controlled by what i ate

a fate of severe sensitivity
discomfort always came upon me

and this was to your knowledge
yet you never acknowledged

still you forced me always
to eat dangerous foods for days

planted them in between meals
sickness you wanted me to feel

— *shifty tactics*

to go against your orders
i was acting like a child
being an immature youth
just in need of a smile

and perhaps i was *disgusting*
a term you so often used
when your desires went unmet
hoping to make my ego bruised

— *manipulation*

was i a fool to think people could change
wishful thinking on my part was strange

— *high hopes*

those long foggy days
always filled with mist
when my mind was adrift

— *lost and confused*

never was there a period of enjoyment
our time together was shaky from
the beginning

never was there a period of peace
with you every moment my head
was spinning

— *foundation of a toxic relationship*

i planned to be free
to feel some liberty
you gripped on tightly
afraid to let go of me

— *holding on*

coercive methods and
countless phone calls
never-ending messages
if only that was all

irregular house visits
odd contact with friends
sporadic moments of stalking
acts that seemed to never end

— *unhealthy behaviour*

i only wanted to let go
get away even though
you were hurt and wounded
as our relationship concluded

— *fading away*

as much time came to pass
you lingered never giving up
whichever path i walked in life
your presence appeared without fail
you watched and followed my moves
and for that i was never able to truly leave

— *the haunting*

some things are not meant to last
forever to be a thought of the past

— *tainted remembrance*

yet even when i found clarity and peace
i had no doubt your shadowing never ceased

— *undesired aftermath*

the last

part four

piers laurent

stuck in my bed staring at the moon
awake all night until the next day at noon

a sentiment of uncertainty forcing me down
painted on my tired face alongside a frown

for long i felt quite a bit of emptiness
thinking a relationship could bring happiness

but my belief attracted the wrong kinds
then misery was all i would find

— insightful

looking back on the choices
and decisions once made
to gain some insight
enlightenment
and vision about myself
what i learned over the years
it was my greatest discovery

— rebirth

going about my days
forging my own way

— personal growth

life had never felt better
a world filled with pleasure

— *turning point*

warm and fuzzy
sensation travelling
through my body

the salubrious air
the budding flowers
no more despair

the lush greenery
the beaming sunlight
everything was right

— *feeling good*

out from nowhere there you came
like a strong gust of wind yet lingering
as a calm breeze on a late summer day

it was at first i thought your presence
was to be only brief like the seasons
but you remained never going away

— *you*

much we had in common from the start
finding one so compatible to myself seemed
near impossible

interests aligned like the stars in the night sky
and our bond grew stronger as the sun rose
each morning

— *true friendship*

the longer you stayed i began to feel
a relaxed sensation i feared was real
though one i needed to figure out
wishing history did not repeat

— *sparks*

how different you were
so unlike all the others
nothing about you was abnormal
odd it was and unpredictable

— *unusual*

i thought it must not be so
for you to not be a problem
yet i kept searching endlessly
like an archaeologist seeking
a lost relic needing to be found

— *digging my own grave*

and then i came to see
your faults right in front of me

yet what i found in you seemed rare
neither dangerous nor disastrous

traits that meshed well with my own
and others that helped me grow

everything was a fragment of you
neither dangerous nor disastrous

— *unearthing*

explosions when our fingers met
hands joined as one with sweat

not even the darkest of nights
could mask the emitting light

— *fireworks*

a melodic composition of voices
produced whenever we conversed
tunes heard from any distance
soothing and playful and just right

— *harmony*

you were a diamond long hidden
one i was not seeking intentionally
but what began as a mere friendship
progressed much more beautifully

— *romance veiled*

the seconds passed so slowly
though never slow enough
all i wanted was for the minutes to stop
to stand still for us to never part
if only the sands of time had stuck
locked at the centre of the hourglass

— *still*

as easy to look at as the clear light sky
yet more calming than the view up high

— *your blue eyes*

lips so grand and rosy
smooth and delicate
whenever i went in closely

eyes a serene scene
calm and tranquil
with a slight gleam

hair so soft and silky
shiny and glossy
of which it was guilty

— *stunning*

like an art piece on display
entrancing in every way

— *unmatched beauty*

that crooked tooth you had
the one you hated so much
the one you wished to fix
i thought it was cute
i thought it was cute
it told a story about you
not everything in life was straight
not everything about you was perfect
but you were who you were
and i adored it all

— *unseen perfection*

an appeal ever so satisfying
i dreamt about you much
something about the way you walked
the way you talked
the way you smiled
left me wanting more and more
like a recreational drug you were
habit-forming
though in a healthy way
oh how i wanted more and more

— *yearning*

what we had was real
something i believed
i had felt before but never did

it was different
with you everything seemed
to be touched with a bit of magic

— *spellbinding*

when the music played loudly
we went about in sync naturally
we manoeuvred around each other
without practice though flawless
like we were destined to do this
for the rest of our lives

— *slow dancing*

any moment was unlike the one before
amazing that i only wanted more
never did i think i would want to be
with someone so much for eternity

— *everlasting*

you found refuge in my arms
as i did in yours

a place of comfort and tranquility
one where we were ourselves

separated from the outside world
that horror and hate and misery

in my arms and in yours
we found what we were looking for

— *home*

you were more
than just amazing
always and forever

you were yourself
and i cherished that
always and forever

— *about you*

together we were meant to go
beyond the plains and the valleys
to walk into the sunset without worry

— hand in hand

intriguing and wonderful
incredible and special
unique and powerful
that innocent thing called love
truly organic and natural
when alive and breathing
the world never ceased to spin

— *love*

eyes closed when drifting to sleep
memories filling my head
past events were life lessons
teachings that masked a blessing

— *reflection*

about the author

piers laurent is a storyteller and poet who can effortlessly capture readers with his eloquent writing. in only a few lines, he can masterfully express the highs and lows of love, loss, and life to ensure that his words are not forgotten long after being read.

about the book

memoir takes readers on a journey of unhealthy relationships and toxic romances. this perceptive collection of poetry documents the suffering faced while searching for love and shows that even the most wounded souls can eventually heal to find what they desire.

www.ingramcontent.com/pod-product-compliance
Lightning Source LLC
Chambersburg PA
CBHW050957050726
47592CB00007B/2614